Success With
Vowels

New York • Toronto • London • Auckland • Sydney
Mexico City • New Delhi • Hong Kong • Buenos Aires

Teaching *Resources*

State Standards Correlations

To find out how this book helps you meet your state's standards, log on to **www.scholastic.com/ssw**

Written by Robin Wolfe
Cover design by Ka-Yeon Kim-Li
Interior illustrations by Kathy Marlin
Interior design by Quack & Company

ISBN-13 978-0-545-20113-1
ISBN-10 0-545-20113-6

Introduction

Understanding phonics is a very important part of learning to read. Parents and teachers alike will find this book to be a valuable tool for teaching beginning readers. The basic skills addressed include recognizing long and short vowels and the sounds they make, learning the rules of vowel patterns, and recognizing some exceptions to the vowel rules.

Children will enjoy playing word games and solving riddles as they complete the activity pages. Puzzles, word finds, and silly rhymes make learning fun. Review pages are included to help teachers and parents assess achievement. Take a look at the Table of Contents and you will feel rewarded providing such a valuable resource for your children. Remember to praise them for their efforts and successes!

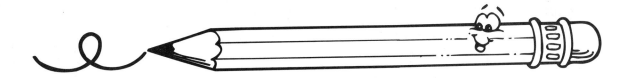

Table of Contents

What Is a Vowel?

There are 26 letters in the alphabet. Five of the letters are **vowels**. They are a, e, i, o, and u.

Look at the alphabet train.

> **Color the *a* car red.**
> **Color the *e* car blue.**
> **Color the *i* car orange.**
> **Color the *o* car purple.**
> **Color the *u* car green.**

Sometimes the letter y can be a vowel.

Color the *y* car yellow.

Look at each store sign. Circle each vowel you can find. There are 13 of them.

Name _____

Abby's Apples

Vowels can make more than one sound. Each vowel has a short sound and a long sound. **Short a** *makes the sound you hear at the beginning of* **apple**. *To help you remember the short-α sound, stretch out the beginning of the word like this:* α-α-α-α-apple.

Abby loves to eat red apples. Help Abby find the red apples that have pictures with the short-*a* sound. Color these apples red. If the picture does not have a short-*a* sound, color the apple green.

 This reptile looks like a crocodile, only smaller. It swims in the water. It begins with the short-*a* sound. What is it? On another sheet of paper, draw one in a zoo.

Fat Cat's Rule

 The consonant-vowel-consonant rule: When only one vowel comes between consonants, that vowel is usually short. To help you remember, mark the short-a sound like this: făt căt.

Unscramble the letters to spell each word. Mark the vowel short.

1. atr _____

2. aht _____

3. ktac _____

4. mkas _____

5. naf _____

6. plam _____

7. pca _____

8. dDa _____

9. tarp _____

10. dahn _____

11. palc _____

12. cklab _____

 This is yucky and smelly! It may be your job to take it out. You put it in a big can or dumpster. Unscramble these letters to find out what it is.

tashr _____ **Mark the vowel short.**

Name _____

 # Short-a Word Families

Look at the word on each paper doll. By changing the first letter, you can make new words. Use the letters below each doll to write the words inside it. Mark each vowel short.

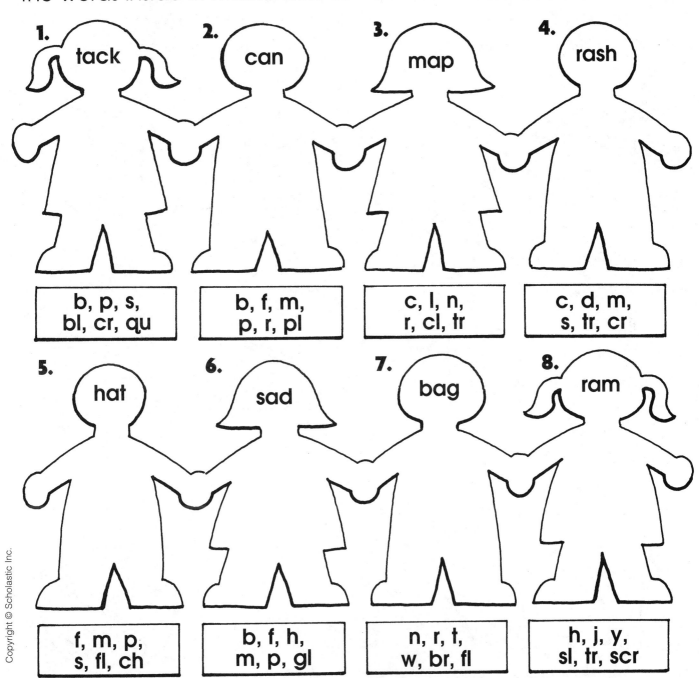

1. tack

b, p, s,
bl, cr, qu

2. can

b, f, m,
p, r, pl

3. map

c, l, n,
r, cl, tr

4. rash

c, d, m,
s, tr, cr

5. hat

f, m, p,
s, fl, ch

6. sad

b, f, h,
m, p, gl

7. bag

n, r, t,
w, br, fl

8. ram

h, j, y,
sl, tr, scr

 This is a car. It rhymes with *lab.* **It is another word for** *taxi.* **What is it? On another sheet of paper, write a story about riding in one.**

Ed's Eggs

 Short e *makes the sound you hear at the beginning of* **egg**. *To help you remember the short-e sound, stretch out the beginning of the word like this:* e-e-e-egg.

It is time for Ed to gather the eggs. Help Ed find the eggs that have pictures with the short-e sound. Color these eggs brown. If the picture does not have the short-e sound, leave the egg white.

 When you say this word you nod your head up and down. It means the opposite of *no*. **It has the short-***e* **sound. What word is it? Think of three questions that you would answer with this word.**

Ned and Ted's Rule

➡ *The consonant-vowel-consonant rule: When only one vowel comes between consonants, that vowel is usually short. To help you remember, mark the short-e sound this way:* Nĕd Tĕd.

Ned and Ted want you to play a picture game. Write the beginning letter of each picture on the blank above it. Read each short-e word that you made. Mark the vowel short.

1. ___ ___ ___ ___

2. ___ ___ ___

3. ___ ___ ___ ___

4. ___ ___ ___

5. ___ ___ ___

6. ___ ___ ___

7. ___ ___ ___ ___

8. ___ ___ ___ ___

9. ___ ___ ___

10. ___ ___ ___ ___

 This person is a doctor for pets. She helps them get well. The word has the short-*e* sound. What is it? Circle the five words in this riddle that have the short-*e* sound. (Be careful! Do not circle any words with the long-*e* sound.)

Short-e Word Jets

Look at the word on each jet. By changing the first letter, you can make new words. Use the letters in the clouds to write new words on the blanks. Mark each vowel short.

This is a tiny, make-believe person. It is like a leprechaun. It rhymes with shelf. What is it? On another sheet of paper, write three sentences about one.

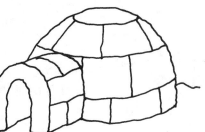

Igloo Inn

 Short i *makes the sound you hear at the beginning of* **igloo**.
*To help you remember the short-*i *sound, stretch out the
beginning of the word like this:* i-i-i-igloo.

Welcome to the Igloo Inn. Outline the pictures with the short-*i*
sound in blue. If the picture does not have a short-*i* sound, draw
an *X* on it.

 **This is part of a baseball game. There are nine of them. The word has two short-*i* sounds.
When you play baseball, someone throws a ball to a batter. This word also has a short-*i*
sound. What are the two words?**

Big Pig's Rule

The consonant-vowel-consonant rule: When only one vowel comes between consonants, that vowel is usually short. To help you remember, mark the short-i sound like this: bĭg pĭg.

Big Pig wants you to practice the rule. In each sentence, underline two words that have the short-i sound. Mark the vowel short. Then write the number of the sentence by the picture that matches it.

1. The twins got on the ship.
2. Hit the ball, Jim!
3. Jack and Jill ran up the hill.
4. The house was made of bricks and sticks.

You can feel it, but you cannot see it. It is invisible. You can tell it is blowing when the trees sway. The word has a short-i sound. What is it?

Short-i Word Lists

Look at the word on each list. By changing the first letter, you can make new words. Write the words on the blanks. Mark each vowel short. Read your words to a friend.

sit

b_____
f_____
h_____
l_____
sp_____
sk_____

dip

h_____
l_____
r_____
s_____
t_____
z_____

lid

b_____
d_____
h_____
k_____
l_____
r_____

big

d_____
f_____
j_____
p_____
r_____
w_____

pin

b_____
f_____
k_____
t_____
w_____
ch_____

kick

l_____
p_____
s_____
t_____
w_____
br_____

will

b_____
f_____
g_____
h_____
m_____
p_____

lift

g_____
r_____
s_____
dr_____
sh_____

You are trying to look at something, but the sun is in your eyes. You squeeze your eyelids almost shut. What is the name for this? The word has a short-*i* sound. Write the word and mark the *i* short. Now show this word with your eyes.

Oliver's Olives

 Short o *makes the sound you hear at the beginning of* **olive.** *To help you remember the short-o sound, stretch out the beginning of the word like this:* o-o-o-olive.

Oliver likes to put green olives in his salad. Help Oliver find the olives that have pictures with the short-*o* sound. Color these olives green. If the picture does not have the short-*o* sound, color the olive black.

 This creature lives in the sea. It has eight arms. Its head looks like a balloon. It begins with the short-*o* sound. What is it? Tell what you could do if you had eight arms!

Top Cop's Rule

 The consonant-vowel-consonant rule: When only one vowel comes between consonants, that vowel is usually short. To help you remember, mark the short-o sound like this: tŏp cŏp.

Look at all the awards this police officer has won! Find the word on the police car that matches each picture. Write the word on the blank. Mark the vowel short.

_____   _____   _____   _____

_____   _____   _____   _____

   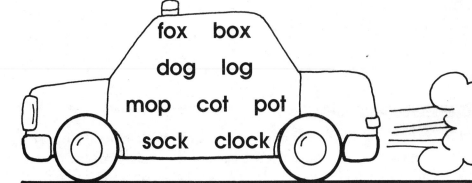

fox   box
dog   log
mop   cot   pot
sock   clock

_____

Short-o Word Socks

Look at the word on each sock. By changing the first letter, you can make new words. Use the letters in the heel of each sock to write the words on the blanks. Mark each vowel short. Read your words to a friend.

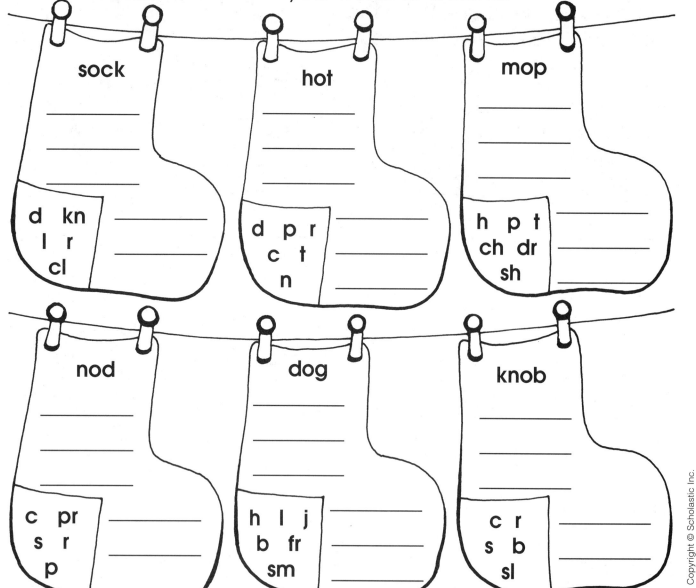

sock

d   kn
l   r
cl

hot

d   p   r
c   t
n

mop

h   p   t
ch   dr
sh

nod

c   pr
s   r
p

dog

h   l   j
b   fr
sm

knob

c   r
s   b
sl

This is a sport. A player hits a small, white ball with a metal club. The player wants the ball to roll on the grass and into a hole. The name of this game has a short-*o* sound. What sport is it? On another sheet of paper, draw a picture of this sport.

Name _____

My Uncle's Umbrella

 Short u *makes the sound you hear at the beginning of* **umbrella**. *To help you remember the short-*u *sound, stretch out the beginning of the word like this:* u-u-u-umbrella.

My uncle needs to buy a new umbrella! Help him find the umbrellas that have pictures with the short-*u* sound. Color these umbrellas with red and blue stripes. If the picture does not have the short-*u* sound, write *NO* on the umbrella.

 This is where rockets go. It is where you look to find the moon. It means the opposite of *down.* **It begins with the short-u sound. What is it? Name five things that can go this way.**

Slug Bug's Rule

The consonant-vowel-consonant rule: When only one vowel comes between consonants, that vowel is usually short. Mark the short u this way to help you remember: slŭg bŭg.

Help Slug Bug get to the flower bed. Circle each word with the short-*u* sound. Mark the vowel short. Then connect the words with the short-*u* sound to help Slug Bug find its way home.

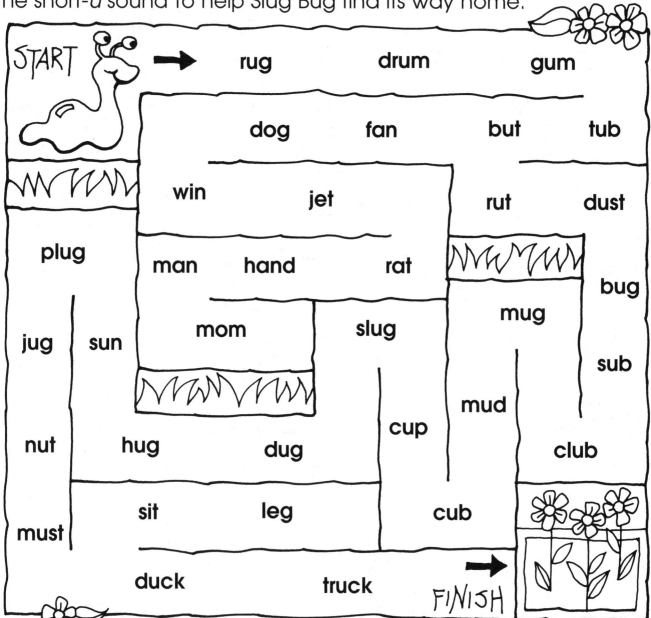

START

rug   drum   gum

dog   fan   but   tub

win   jet   rut   dust

plug   man   hand   rat

bug

mug

jug   sun   mom   slug

sub

nut   hug   dug   mud   club

cup

must   sit   leg   cub

duck   truck   FINISH

 This word can mean a male deer, or it can be another name for a dollar. It has the short-*u*** sound. What is it? On another sheet of paper, write the word and draw a picture of both meanings.**

Name _____

Short-u Word Rugs

Look at the word on each rug. By changing the first letter, you can make new words. Write the words on the blanks. Mark each vowel short. Read your words to a friend.

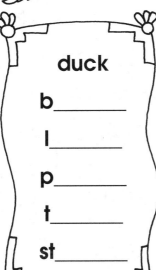

rug

b_____

d_____

h_____

m_____

t_____

duck

b_____

l_____

p_____

t_____

st_____

mud

b_____

c_____

d_____

sp_____

th_____

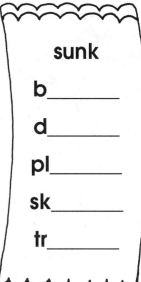

sunk

b_____

d_____

pl_____

sk_____

tr_____

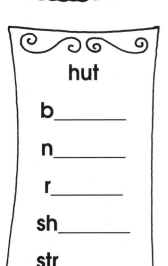

hut

b_____

n_____

r_____

sh_____

str_____

sung

h_____

l_____

r_____

fl_____

st_____

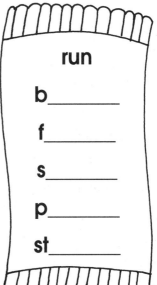

run

b_____

f_____

s_____

p_____

st_____

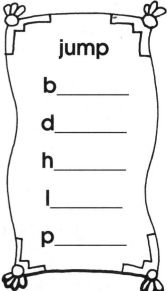

jump

b_____

d_____

h_____

l_____

p_____

 This stuff settles on the furniture. It sticks to the TV screen. You can clean it off with a rag. The word has the short-u sound. It rhymes with *rust*. What is it? On another sheet of paper, draw a robot that can do this job for you!

Al and Ed's Rule

 The vowel-consonant rule: When a two-letter word begins with a vowel, the vowel is usually short. To help you remember, mark the short vowels this way:

ăd Ăl ăm ăn Ĕd ăs ăt ĭf ĭn ĭs ĭt ŏn ŏx ŭp ŭs

Al and Ed are talking on the phone. Read what they are saying. Every time you see one of the words from above, underline it and mark the vowel short. Some words are used twice.

Al: Hello? Is this Ed?

Ed: Yes, it is.

Al: I saw your ad in the paper. Are you selling an ox?

Ed: Yes, I am. Come to my barn if you want to see him.

Al: Is it the big red barn on Pine Tree Lane?

Ed: Yes, turn left at the lake. Then go up the hill.

Al: Okay, I will be there as soon as I can.

Ed: Fine. You will find us in the pen behind the barn.

Al: Good-bye.

Ed: Good-bye.

 This is a tool used to chop down trees. It has a short-*a* sound and a consonant. What is it? On another sheet of paper, draw one.

Testing, Testing, 1-2-3

Say the name of each picture. Fill in the circle under the word that matches the picture. Mark the vowel short.

	bag ○	bud ○	bed ○		skill ○	skunk ○	chunk ○
	will ○	well ○	bell ○		jam ○	get ○	jet ○
	fan ○	can ○	fin ○		crib ○	bib ○	big ○
	best ○	fast ○	fist ○		at ○	ox ○	ax ○
	man ○	mad ○	can ○		cash ○	truck ○	trash ○
	bog ○	box ○	beg ○		bug ○	bunk ○	bus ○
	deck ○	duck ○	dock ○		ship ○	shop ○	dish ○

 Both of these snacks are fun to eat at a party. You use one of them to scoop up the other one. Then you eat them together. Both words have a short-*i* sound. What are they? Plan a pretend party. What will you serve? On another sheet of paper, make a list.

Amy's Aprons

 Every vowel has a long sound and a short sound. **Long a** *makes the sound you hear at the beginning of* **apron**. *To help remember the long-*a *sound, stretch out the beginning of the word like this:* a-a-a-a-apron.

Amy needs a new apron. Help Amy find the aprons that have pictures with the long-*a* sound. Color these aprons pink. If the picture on an apron does not have a long-*a* sound, color it purple.

 There is a first one, a second one, and a third one. When you hit the baseball, you run and step on them. The word has the long-*a* sound. What is it? On another sheet of paper, draw a baseball field. Draw arrows that point to your answer.

The Bake-a-Cake Rule

 The consonant-vowel-consonant-silent e *rule: When a word ends in a silent* e, *the vowel that comes before the* e *will be long and will say its name. To help you remember, mark the long* a *and silent* e *this way:* bāké cāké.

It is fun to bake a cake! Read the words on the bowls. Mark the vowels in each word like the examples above. Then draw a line to match the word to the correct picture on the cake.

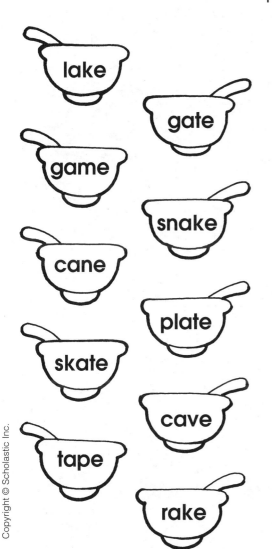

lake

gate

game

snake

cane

plate

skate

cave

tape

rake

 You can find 50 of them on a U.S. map. Utah is one. Texas is one. The word has a long-*a* **sound and silent** *e* **in it. What is it ? Look at a U.S. map and see if you can find yours.**

The Bait-and-Wait Rule

 The consonant-vowel-vowel-consonant rule: When two vowels come together, the first vowel is usually long, and the second vowel is silent. You can say it this way, "When two vowels go walking, the first one does the talking!" To help you remember, mark the a long and the next vowel silent like this: bāit wāit.

A person fishing must bait a hook and then wait for a fish to bite. Color each fish with the long-*a* sound in blue. Then mark the vowels in each word like the examples above. If a word does not have the long-*a* sound, color it orange.

paid

ant

brain

mail

rain

pant

maid

egg

nail

snail

paint

train

 This is the name for little round balls of ice that fall during a storm. Bigger ones can make dents in cars. The word has a long-*a* sound in it. What is it? On another sheet of paper, draw a picture of it.

Name _____

Long-a Word Snakes

Look at the word on each basket. By changing the first letter, you can make new words. Use the letters on each snake to help you. Write the words on the blanks below each snake. Mark each *a* long. Cross out any silent letters.

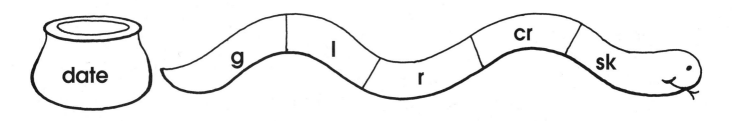

date — g   l   r   cr   sk

_____ _____ _____ _____ _____

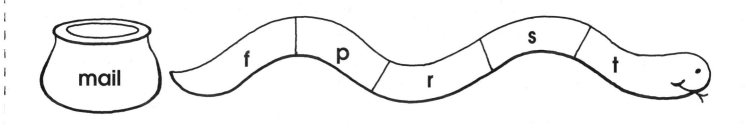

mail — f   p   r   s   t

_____ _____ _____ _____ _____

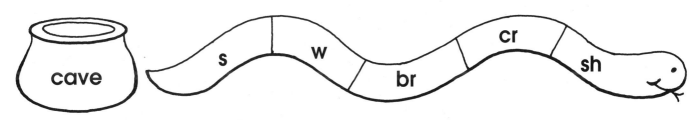

cave — s   w   br   cr   sh

_____ _____ _____ _____ _____

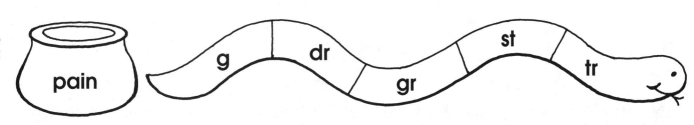

pain — g   dr   gr   st   tr

_____ _____ _____ _____ _____

Ethan's Eagle

Long e *makes the sound you hear at the beginning of* **eagle**. *To help you remember the long-e sound, stretch out the beginning of the word like this:* e-e-e-eagle.

Ethan's eagle is lonely. He needs a friend. Help Ethan find the eagles that have pictures with the long-e sound. Color these eagles brown. If the picture on an eagle does not have a long-e sound, write *NO* on it.

 You have one of these on the end of your pencil. It is made of rubber. You need it when you make a mistake! It begins with the long-*e* sound. What is it? Write your name with a pencil. Now rub it off with the answer to the riddle.

Pete's Rule

 The consonant-vowel-consonant-silent e *rule: When a word ends in a silent* e, *the vowel that comes before the* e *will be long and will say its name. To help you remember, mark the long* e *and silent* e *this way:* Pēté.

There are not many words that have a long *e* and a silent *e* in them, but you can find one in each scrambled sentence below. Write the words in the correct order on the line. Use the pictures to help you.

1. dog. is Zeke my

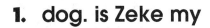

2. tulips. The is theme

3. baked Irene cookies.

4. coach. is Gene my

5. these. like do I not

6. Steve goal. a scored

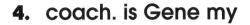

 This a nonsense word— zepe. Mark the first *e* **long and the last** *e* **silent. Now think up a funny meaning for the word. On another sheet of paper, write a sentence using the word and draw a picture about it.**

The Sweet Treat Rule

The consonant-vowel-vowel-consonant rule: When two vowels come together, the first vowel is usually long and the second vowel is silent. You can say, "When two vowels go walking, the first one does the talking!" To help you remember, mark the e long and the next vowel silent, like this: sweet treat.

Look at the sweet treats below. In each box, write the number of the word that matches the picture. Then mark each word like the examples above.

1. **sheep**

2. **teeth**

3. **feet**

4. **leaf**

5. **beads**

6. **wheel**

7. **green beans**

8. **seal**

9. **jeans**

10. **meat**

11. **team**

 This is part of your foot. It is not your toes. It is the other end. It has the long-*e* sound. What is it? On another sheet of paper, trace around your foot. Draw an arrow pointing to your answer.

Name _____

Long-e Word Wheels

Look at the word in the middle of each wheel. By changing the first letter, you can make new words. Write the words on the wheels. Mark each e long. Cross out any silent letters. Read your words to a friend.

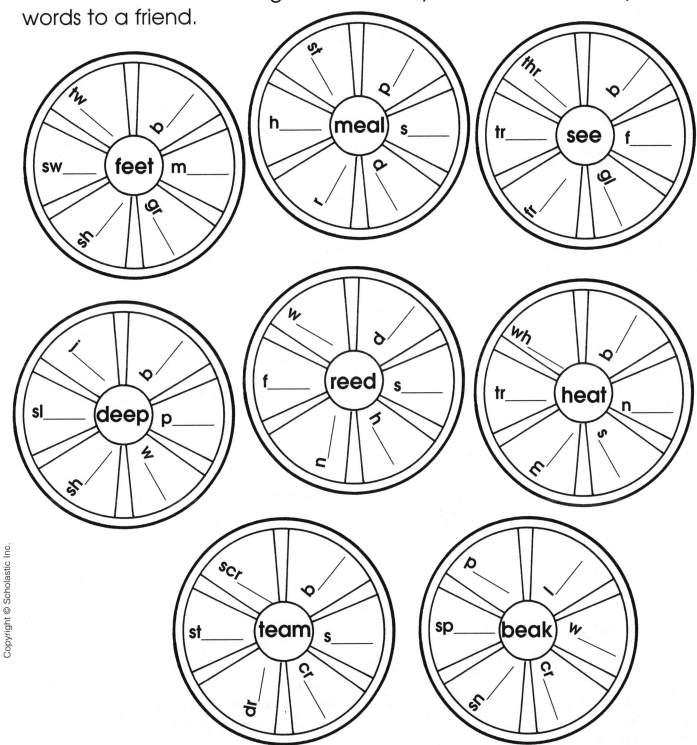

Ivan's Ice

 Long i *makes the sound you hear at the beginning of* **ice**. *To help you remember the long-i sound, stretch out the beginning of the word like this:* i-i-i-ice.

It is so hot today! Ivan needs some ice in his drink. Help Ivan find the ice cubes that have pictures with the long-*i* sound. Outline these ice cubes in blue. If the picture on an ice cube does not have a long-*i* sound, draw a puddle of water around it to make it look like it is melting.

 This is something your lips do when you are happy. It is another word for *grin*. **It has the long-*i* sound. What is it? On another sheet of paper, draw a picture of your face with one of these on it.**

Name _____

The Nice Mice Rule

 The consonant-vowel-consonant-silent e rule: When a word ends in a silent e, the vowel that comes before the e will be long and will say its name. To help you remember, mark the long i and silent e this way: nīce̸ mīce̸.

Two nice mice have made a game for you to play. Say the name of each picture. Circle the correct word. Mark the long *i* and the silent *e* like the examples above.

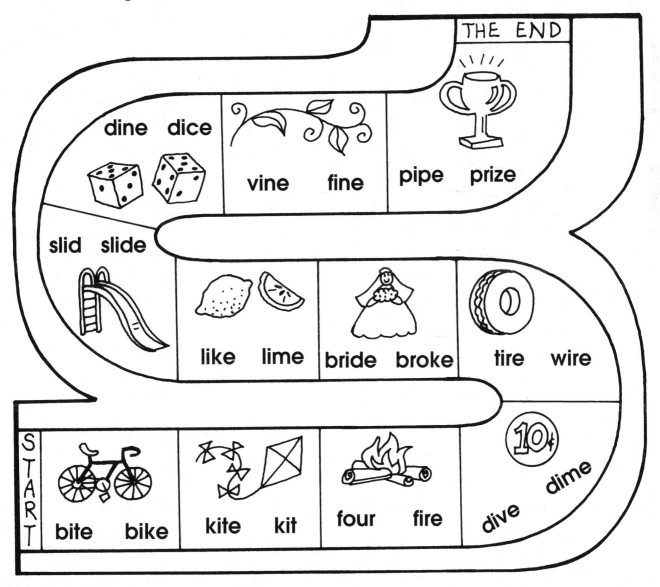

dine   dice

vine   fine

pipe   prize

THE END

slid   slide

like   lime

bride   broke

tire   wire

bite   bike

kite   kit

four   fire

dive   dime

 On another sheet of paper, write the number words from one to ten. Find two words that have a long *i* and a silent *e*. What are they?

Long-i Word Slides

Look at the word on each slide. By changing the first letter, you can make new words. Write the words on the slide. Mark each *i* long. Cross out any silent letters. Read your words to a friend.

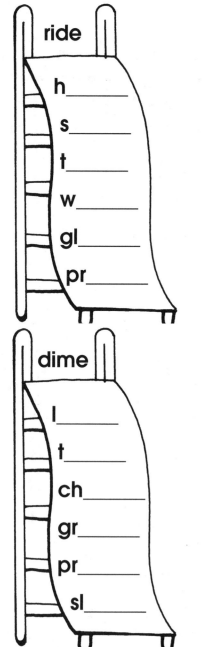

ride

h_____
s_____
t_____
w_____
gl_____
pr_____

mice

n_____
r_____
pr_____
sl_____
sp_____
tw_____

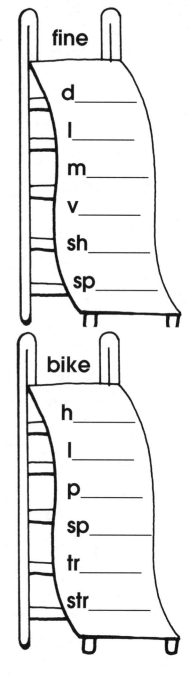

fine

d_____
l_____
m_____
v_____
sh_____
sp_____

dime

l_____
t_____
ch_____
gr_____
pr_____
sl_____

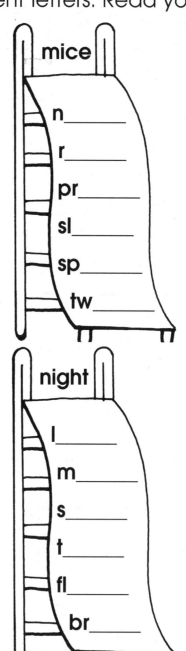

night

l_____
m_____
s_____
t_____
fl_____
br_____

bike

h_____
l_____
p_____
sp_____
tr_____
str_____

This is the name for a woman who is married. It is the opposite of husband. It has a long-*i* sound. What is the word? Change the first letter to *l* to make a rhyming word.

Miss Ova's Ovals

 Long o *makes the sound you hear at the beginning of* **oval**. *To help you remember the long-o sound, stretch out the beginning of the word like this:* o-o-o-oval.

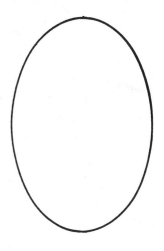

Miss Ova is teaching her class about shapes. Today they learned about ovals. Draw an oval around the pictures that have the long-*o* sound. If the picture does not have a long-*o* sound, draw a square around it.

 You might see this word on a sign in the window of a store. It lets you know you can go inside. It is the opposite of *closed*. **It begins with a long-o sound. What is the word? On another sheet of paper, make one of these signs and decorate it.**

The Bone-in-the-Stone Rule

The consonant-vowel-consonant-silent e rule: When a word ends in a silent e, the vowel that comes before the e will be long and will say its name. To help you remember, mark the long o and silent e this way: bōne stōne.

Look at the words in the bones below. Mark each long o and silent e like the examples above. Then finish each picture to show the words.

a yellow rose

smoke in the air

a hot stove

a stepping stone

a big red nose

a home for them

a globe for her

a water hose

a long rope

This is something you can wear over your pajamas. It keeps you warm on cold nights. You take it off before you go to bed. It has a long o and a silent e. What is it? On another sheet of paper, draw and color one with stripes.

The Float-a-Boat Rule

The consonant-vowel-vowel-consonant rule: When two vowels come together, the first vowel is usually long and the second vowel is silent. You can say it this way, "When two vowels go walking, the first one does the talking!" To help you remember, mark the o long and the next vowel silent like this: flōat bōat.

Look at all the boats! Find the word that matches the picture and write it on the blank. Then mark the vowels in each word like the example above.

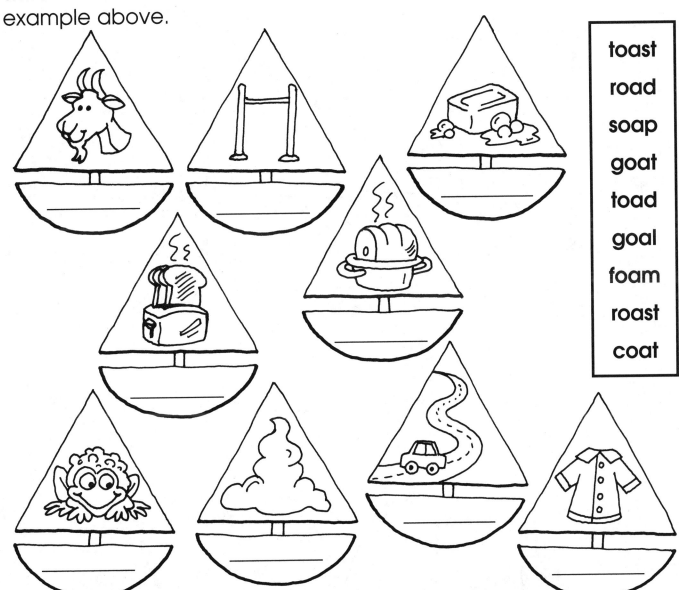

| toast |
| road |
| soap |
| goat |
| toad |
| goal |
| foam |
| roast |
| coat |

The word *croak* has a long *o* and silent *a*. What is another word with a long *o* and silent *a* that names an animal that makes a croak sound?

Long-o Word Soap

Look at the word on each bar of soap. By changing the first letter, you can make new words. Use the letters in the bubbles to write the words on the soap. Mark each *o* long. Cross out any silent letters. Read your words to a friend.

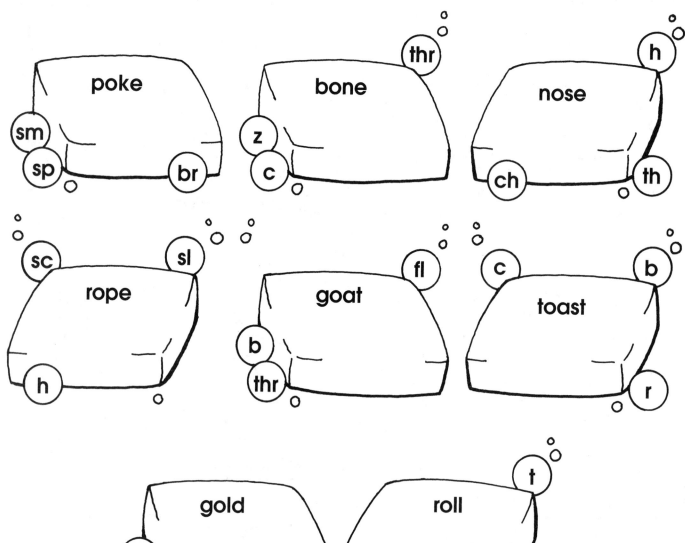

poke
sm
sp
br

bone
thr
z
c

nose
h
ch
th

rope
sc
sl
h

goat
fl
b
thr

toast
c
b
r

gold
h
b
sc

roll
t
scr
str

Unicorn University

 Long u *makes the sound you hear at the beginning of* **unicorn.** *To help you remember the long-*U *sound, stretch out the beginning of the word like this:* U-U-U-Unicorn.

This unicorn is smart! He goes to Unicorn University. Find every book that has a picture with the long-*u* sound. Color these books blue. If the picture does not have a long-*u* sound, draw an *X* on it.

1. Turn in your work.
2. No talking in class.
3. Raise your hand.
4. Keep your desk clean.

 This is the name of a country. It is made up of 50 states. Its president lives in Washington, D.C. The first word begins with a long-*u* sound. What country is it? On another sheet of paper, draw the flag of this country.

Mr. Mule's Rule

 The consonant-vowel-consonant-silent e rule: When a word ends in a silent e, the vowel that comes before the e will be long and will say its name. To help you remember, mark the long u and silent e like this: mūlǿ rūlǿ.

Mr. Mule has all the answers! He wants you to choose one of his words to complete each sentence. Write the word on the blank and mark the vowels like the example above.

chute   huge   rude
dune   flute   June
cute

1. It is _____ to talk back to your mother.

2. She plays the _____ in the band.

3. Throw your dirty socks down the clothes _____.

4. It is fun to roll down a big sand _____.

5. The giant had _____ feet!

6. My birthday is in _____.

7. This baby is so _____!

This is what toothpaste comes in. You squeeze it to get some out. It has a little top that screws on. It has a long u and a silent e. What is it? Write the word and mark the vowels.

Long-u Word Fruit

Look at the word on each piece of fruit. Change the first letter to make a rhyming word. Write the word on the blank. Mark each *u* long. Cross out any silent letters. Read your words to a friend.

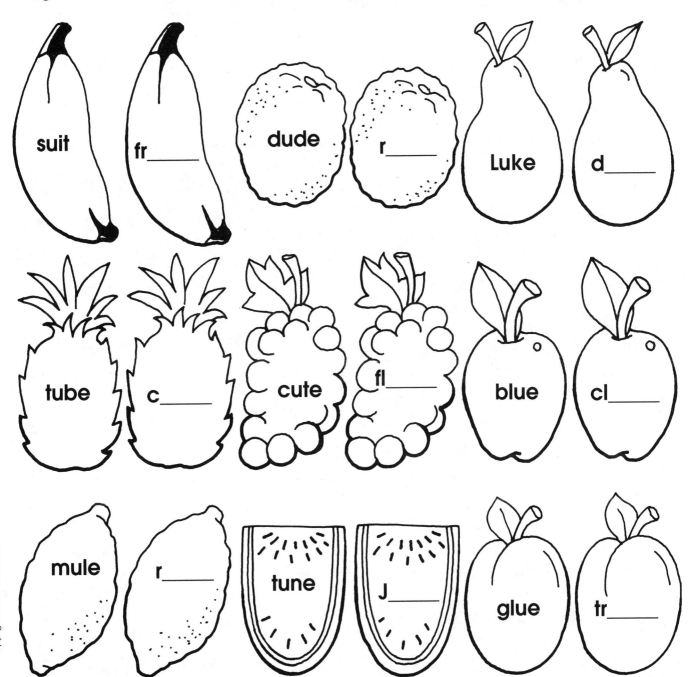

suit   fr_____   dude   r_____   Luke   d_____

tube   c_____   cute   fl_____   blue   cl_____

mule   r_____   tune   J_____   glue   tr_____

💡 **This is the color of the sky and the sea. It has a long-u sound. What is it? Think of something else that is this color. On another sheet of paper, draw and color it.**

Jo Jo's Rule

 The consonant-vowel rule: When a little word ends in a vowel, it is usually long. To help you remember, mark the long vowels this way:

hē	**shē**	**wē**	**mē**	**bē**	**hī**	**gō**	**nō**	**sō**

Look at the picture. Use the words in the box to finish the story. Write your answers on the blanks. Remember to mark each vowel long.

No, I am sorry. We have to go.

Hi! Will you play with me?

Jo Jo thought it would __ __   __ __ much fun to play at the park. Jo Jo said,

"__ __! Will you play with __ __?"

__ __ said, "__ __, I am sorry. __ __ have to __ __."

Poor Jo Jo! __ __ __ needs a friend!

Now color the picture. Read the story to a friend.

Kay and Jay's Rule

 The consonant-ay rule: When a word ends in ay, the a is long and the y is silent.
To help you remember, mark the vowels this way: Kāy̸ Jāy̸.

Hi kids! To join Kay and Jay's club, add these consonants to the letters *ay* to make new words. Write the words on the clubhouse. The first one is done for you.

m	s	pl	w	tr	gr	d	r
p	st	spr	h	l	b	sw	

may

Club Rule:
When a word ends in *ay*, the *a* is long and the *y* is silent.

 What word did you make that is something for horses to eat?

Long-Vowel Pizzas

Look at the picture on each slice of pizza. Draw a circle around the word that matches the picture. Then mark the vowels in your answer.

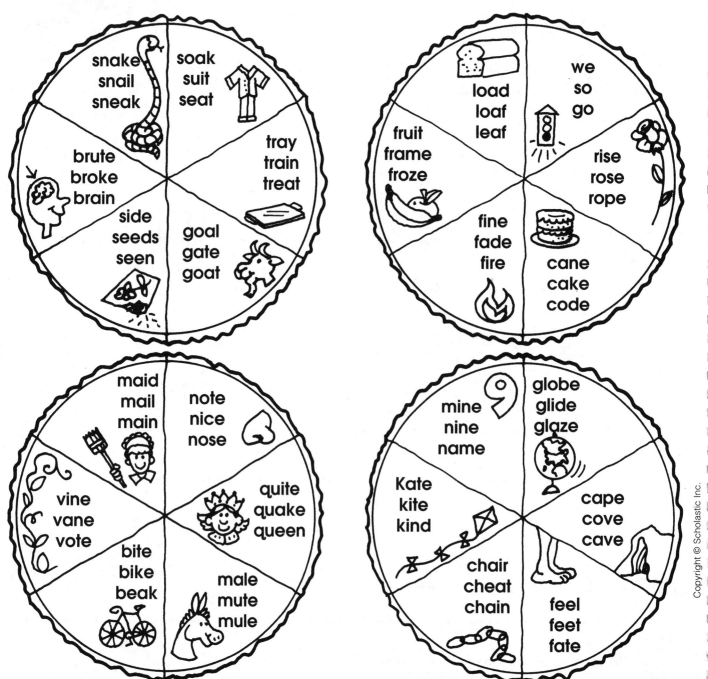

Pizza 1:

- snake / snail / sneak
- soak / suit / seat
- tray / train / treat
- brute / broke / brain
- side / seeds / seen
- goal / gate / goat

Pizza 2:

- load / loaf / leaf
- we / so / go
- fruit / frame / froze
- rise / rose / rope
- fine / fade / fire
- cane / cake / code

Pizza 3:

- maid / mail / main
- note / nice / nose
- quite / quake / queen
- vine / vane / vote
- bite / bike / beak
- male / mute / mule

Pizza 4:

- mine / nine / name
- globe / glide / glaze
- cape / cove / cave
- Kate / kite / kind
- chair / cheat / chain
- feel / feet / fate

 **Cloudy Sky**

When y comes at the beginning of a word, it has a consonant sound as in **yarn**. However, when y comes at the end of a word, it can make the long-e sound as in **cloudy**, or it can make the long-i sound as in **sky**.

Say the name of each picture below. Decide if the y in each word has the long-e sound or the long-i sound. Write each word in the correct cloud. Use the word list to help you.

cloudy:
long-e sound

sky:
long-i sound

puppy
cherry
cry
baby
fry
windy
penny
fly
candy

This special y comes in the middle of a word. It sounds like a short i. What word has a y in the middle and means a building where basketball games are played? What else can you play there?

Short-Vowel Outlaws

 The consonant-vowel-consonant rule is: When only one vowel comes between consonants, that vowel is usually short. They are "the good guys." However, some words do not follow the rules. These words are the "outlaws."

What is the best way to figure out a word you do not know? First, see if it follows the rule. If that does not make a real word, then try other vowel sounds until the word makes sense.

Write the words that have the short vowel sound in the boxes under the "good guy." Write the words that do not follow the rule in the boxes under the "outlaw."

cặt   pĭg   dŏg

ball   wild   cold

fan	climb	mop	child	post
watch	bank	pot	mind	roll

Copyright © Scholastic Inc.

Long-Vowel Outlaws

The consonant-vowel-consonant-silent e rule is: When a word ends in a silent e, the vowel that comes before the e will be long and will say its name. These words are "the good guys." However, some words do not follow the rules. These words are "the outlaws."

What is the best way to figure out a word you do not know? First, see if it follows the rule. If that does not make a real word, then try other vowel sounds until the word makes sense.

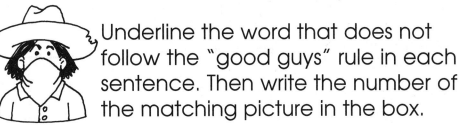

Underline the word that does not follow the "good guys" rule in each sentence. Then write the number of the matching picture in the box.

cāvé	I have curly hair.	☐
dīvé	Bees give us honey.	☐
stōvé	I love my new gloves.	☐
	Let's move to the city.	☐
bōné	I am glad winter is gone.	☐
pāsté	Watch my puppet dance!	☐
Pēté	There is a dog behind the fence.	☐

I Am Long! I Am Short!

Read the words in each picture frame. Two words have a long-vowel sound. Mark the vowels in these words. One word has a short-vowel sound. Circle it. The first one has been done for you.

bāit
(bat)
bāke

mail
made
mad

play
pay
pan

can
cane
case

fake
fan
faint

rug
June
suit

no
me
at

boat
bone
box

fast
stay
day

Steve
Tom
Gene

milk
mile
main

face
fun
flute

vote
soap
six

hi
if
we

home
feet
big

dog
dive
date

Page 5
short-a words: cat, hat, flag, ant, ham, map, sack, hand;
alligator

Page 6
1. rat; 2. hat; 3. tack; 4. mask; 5. fan; 6. lamp; 7. cap; 8. Dad; 9. trap; 10. hand; 11. clap; 12. black;
trash

Page 7
1. back, pack, sack, black, crack, quack; 2. ban, fan, man, pan, ran, plan; 3. cap, lap, nap, rap, clap, trap; 4. cash, dash, mash, sash, trash, crash; 5. fat, mat, pat, sat, flat, chat; 6. bad, fad, had, mad, pad, glad; 7. nag, rag, tag, wag, brag, flag; 8. ham, jam, yam, slam, tram, scram;
cab

Page 8
short-e words: leg, net, belt, desk, neck, ten, sled, nest;
yes

Page 9
1. sled; 2. leg; 3. bell; 4. bed; 5. jet; 6. net; 7. rest; 8. test; 9. pet; 10. desk;
vet; pets, helps, them, get, well

Page 10
fell, tell, well, yell; get, met, net, pet; best, nest, test, vest; bent, tent, sent, rent; fed, red, led, wed; peck, neck, speck, check; den, ten, pen, men;
elf

Page 11
short-i words: chick, pig, fish, bib, chin, ship, pin, six;
innings, pitcher

Page 12
1. The twins got on the ship.
2. Hit the ball, Jim!
3. Jack and Jill ran up the hill.
4. The house was made of bricks and sticks.;
2, 4, 3, 1;
wind

Page 13
bit, fit, hit, lit, spit, skit; hip, lip, rip, sip, tip, zip; bid, did, hid, kid, lid, rid; dig, fig, jig, pig, rig, wig; bin, fin, kin, tin, win, chin; lick, pick, sick, tick, wick, brick; bill, fill, gill, hill, mill, pill; gift, rift, sift, drift, shift;
squint

Page 14
short-o words: mop, hot, hop, log, sock, dog, frog, clock;
octopus

Page 15
fox, box, sock, dog, log, mop, cot, pot, clock

Page 16
dock, knock, lock, rock, clock; dot, pot, rot, cot, tot, not; hop, pop, top, chop, drop, shop; cod, prod, sod, rod, pod; hog, log, jog, bog, frog, smog; cob, rob, sob, bob, slob;
golf

Page 17
short-u words: drum, plug, duck, bug, rug, gum, sun, sub;
up

Page 18
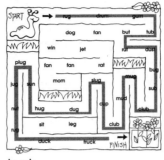
buck

Page 19
bug, dug, hug, mug, tug; buck, luck, puck, tuck, stuck; bud, cud, dud, spud, thud; bunk, dunk, plunk, skunk, trunk; but, nut, rut, shut, strut; hung, lung, rung, flung, stung; bun, fun, sun, pun, stun; bump, dump, hump, lump, pump;
dust

Page 20
Al: Hello? Is this Ed?

Ed: Yes, it is.

Al: I saw your ad in the paper. Are you selling an ox?

Ed: Yes, I am. Come to my barn if you want to see him.

Al: Is it the big red barn on Pine Tree Lane?

Ed: Yes, turn left at the lake. Then go up the hill.

Al: Okay, I will be there as soon as I can.

Ed: Fine. You will find us in the pen behind the barn.

Al: Good-bye.

Ed: Good-bye.;
ax

Page 21
bed, skunk; well, jet; fan, bib; fist, ax; man, trash; box, bus; duck, ship;
chips and dip

Page 22
snake, rain, vase, rake, chain, cake, game, plate, paint;
base

Page 23
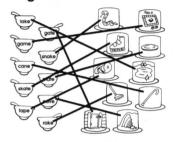
state

Page 24
paid, brain, rain, mail, maid, nail, snail, paint, train;
hail

Page 25
gate, late, rate, crate, skate; fail, pail, rail, sail, tail; save, wave, brave, crave, shave; gain, drain, grain, stain, train

Page 26
wheel, feet, meat, teeth, peach, queen, sheep, key;
eraser

Page 27
1. Zeke is my dog. 2. The theme is tulips. 3. Irene baked cookies. 4. Gene is my coach. 5. I do not like these. 6. Steve scored a goal.

Page 28

heel

Page 29

beet, meet, greet, sheet, sweet, tweet; steal, peal, seal, deal, real, heal; bee, fee, glee, free, tree, three; beep, peep, weep, sheep, sleep, jeep; deed, seed, heed, need, feed, weed; beat, neat, seat, meat, treat, wheat; beam, seam, cream, dream, steam, scream; leak, weak, creak, sneak, speak, peak

Page 30

kite, tie, iron, fly, pie, bike, slide, tire, dice; smile

Page 31

bike, kite, fire, dime, tire, bride, lime, slide, dice, vine, prize; five, nine

Page 32

hide, side, tide, wide, glide, pride; nice, rice, price, slice, spice, twice; dine, line, mine, vine, shine, spine; lime, time, chime, grime, prime, slime; light, might, sight, tight, flight, bright; hike, like, pike, spike, trike, strike; wife, life

Page 33

rope, coat, soap, snow, bone, toe, boat, goat; open

Page 34

Check children's illustrations.; robe

Page 35

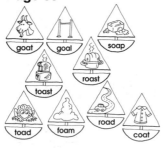

toad

Page 36

smoke, spoke, broke; throne, zone, cone; hose, chose, those; scope, slope, hope; float, boat, throat; coast, boast, roast; hold, bold, scold; toll, scroll, stroll

Page 37

flute, glue, mule, fruit, bruise, juice, suit, rules; United States of America

Page 38

1. rude; 2. flute; 3. chute; 4. dune; 5. huge; 6. June; 7. cute; tube

Page 39

fruit, rude, duke; cube, flute, clue; rule, June, true; blue

Page 40

Jo Jo thought it would be so much fun to play at the park. Jo Jo said, "Hi! Will you play with me?" He said, "No, I am sorry. We have to go." Poor Jo Jo! She needs a friend!

Page 41

say, play, way, tray, gray, day, ray, pay, stay, spray, hay, lay, bay, sway; hay

Page 42

snake, suit, tray, goat, seeds, brain; loaf, go, rose, cake, fire, fruit; maid, nose, queen, mule, bike, vine; nine, globe, cave, feet, chain, kite

Page 43

long-e sound: baby, cherry, puppy, candy, windy, penny; long-i sound: fly, fry, cry; gym

Page 44

short vowels word: fan, bank, mop, pot; exceptions to the rule: climb, child, post, watch, mind, roll

Page 45

cavē	I have curly hair.	4
dīvē	Bees give us honey.	2
stōvē	I love my new gloves.	1
	Let's move to the city.	6
bōnē	I am glad winter is gone.	5
pāstē	Watch my puppet dance!	3
Pētē	There is a dog behind the fence.	7

4, 2, 1, 6, 5, 3, 7

Page 46